What is it?..

Some people have **it**, some don't. Those who have **it**, take **it** for granted, assuming **it** is common sense possessed by all.

With **it** . . . you read situations astutely. You get included and invited, creating powerful alliances that guide and protect.

Without **it** . . . you mis-read signals, count on people who won't come through, work harder and get rewarded less.

What is **it**? **It** is that mind-set called savvy; the awareness and understanding of people and systems.

Savvy is not formally taught but acquired, often through the school of hard-knocks. Acquiring savvy is an internal process; it is the synthesis of information, experience and choice.

I picture savvy people with invisible antenna, scanning the environment, alerting them to danger and opportunity. Like radar, it aids in navigating the unknown.

Savvy has always been essential for success, but players and the game they played used to be easier to identify.

Savvy is even more important today because the games are more competitive, more global, more culturally specific. The players need to be more flexible, more capable of working with diverse people in diverse settings.

What is **it** that will help you identify the game, the players and the rules?

. . . SAVVY

What People Say About Billi. And Her Message:

"I would recommend you to any company to help their employees get the clear message you send on business survival in the 90's and beyond."
Dennis Culver, Senior Vice President
Norwest Mortgage, Inc.

"Your keynote address . . . really kicked off the conference in an upbeat way!
Susan Fronk, Vice President

"Your presentation . . . was awesome. This was perhaps the twentieth time I have seen you in action and have seen thousands respond—Billi you are better than ever!!! People who were ineffective . . . are functioning very smoothly—overnight!
Don T. Floyd, Jr., Chief Operating Officer
National 4-H Council

"Thought you might enjoy feedback on the impression you made. Our chief mill boss attended your session with great reluctance, predetermined it would be a total waste of time . . . next morning he told me he couldn't believe . . . the dramatic improvement in interdepartmental relations."
Converse B. Smith, Regional Vice President
Wisconsin Paperboard

"If people will listen to what you have to say, a lot of EEO complaints, lawsuits, etc. would never occur."
April Fletcher, Manager

Other Products
By
Billi Lee

"Success Savvy" Audio Package

"Success Savvy" Seminars

"Team Savvy" Workshops

"On Track" Team Coaching

"Executive Savvy" Personal Coaching

Keynote Speeches

ATTENTION: Organizations and Corporations

Most of Billi Lee and Company, Inc. books and products are available at special quantity discounts for bulk purchases for sales promotions, premiums or fund-raising. For information please contact us:

billilee@billilee.com

www.billilee.com

SAVVY
Thirty Days to a Different Perspective

Billi Lee

Edited by
Marla M. Koupal

Published by:
Alliance Press, Inc.
Contact: billilee@billilee.com

Savvy . . . Thirty Days To A Different Perspective

Billi Lee and Company, Inc.
www.billilee.com
billilee@billilee.com

Illustrations by Laura VanTine

Printed and bound in the United States of America

To my mother, Marian Vosburgh, for the love,
freedom . . . and courage to invest.

SPECIAL THANKS

To Dana Smith and Marla Koupal for the magic they produce.

To Marty Lee, husband extraordinaire, for the support and space to play my game.

To Vanessa, my delightful daughter, who encourages her mother to do what she has to do.

To my friends who believed years ago.

To the clients, students and radio listeners who also teach.

Preface

You'll love this book! I did when I saw the original draft. It was refreshing to have someone writing about the way I like to operate.

Editing this book was a challenge that only those of you who have heard Billi speak live can understand. Transforming her dynamic speaking style into a book that retains her humorous and fresh approach kept me up late many nights.

The message was so inspiring and thought provoking it was hard to sleep anyway.

I know the message works, I've seen it change the perspectives of our clients and course participants. When you try out some of the ideas, you may feel a bit like Indiana Jones . . . stepping off the cliff. In the movie it appeared as if he was stepping into thin air, but if you remember, he landed on a log below.

The supporting philosophy in this book and savvy strategies will be your "log" when you jump off your cliffs.

Collaborating with Billi is exciting, it is the essence of what we teach. To be effective you need to align yourself with savvy people who work smart.

It was fun to try on an "editing hat" for this project . . . a new cliff for me. It will also be fun to resume my marketing and training projects. Uh-oh, as I finish this . . . Billi just handed me another rough manuscript.

Marla M. Koupal, Editor

Introduction

About this book:

It was written after years of telling people, "No, I don't have a book . . . yet"; after too many people with money in hand tried to buy it; after too many smart, savvy people looked me in the eye and said "write it".

It is the result of teaching and learning from thousands of participants in seminars I've conducted. It can't replace the experience of a live, dynamic class where the students also teach the teacher, but it contains the basics on how to play well.

About the author:

I grew up in a small midwestern town where hard work and talent helped me overcome a significant lack of money and helped me work my way through school. I was blessed with a touch of arrogance that led me to believe I could do anything I wanted . . . as long as I paid for it.

Hard work also enabled me to have my first restaurant at the age of 19 which paid for a year of study in France. I earned two degrees in four years while working 30 hours a week. These early achievements only contributed to my arrogance . . . I thought I knew the road to success.

I signed up with the Peace Corp to fix the world. They sent me to Zaire, Africa where my arrogance met my lack of experience and savvy. I found out I didn't know it all. My education included being held hostage for three days at Entebbe airport, "arrested" by local officials looking for hand-outs, and generally ignored by the people I was sent to teach.

I returned to American humbled. But once again hard work paid off. I acquired two more restaurants, developed a successful direct sales organization, preached the gospel of positive thinking in my motivational seminars, accomplished a bankruptcy and watched other people, no smarter or harder - working than myself, move ahead.

Then I began to "get it". I met a brilliant woman, named Lida "Jinx" Melia who presented courses with a different perspective, full of uncommon common sense. We resonated and I discovered my calling.

So began a ten year journey, studying, learning and teaching ideas on how to be effective. I've taught hundreds of seminars and delivered countless keynote speeches. I've been privileged to have been coached by the best players in the world. People from every kind of organization have contributed to my understanding of their cultures. They've shared their personal stories, enlightened and entertained me.

Working in Russia and Australia, this last year, I discovered that cultures may change, the size and shape of the court may change . . . but the game remains the same.

The philosophy behind the ideas in this book is universal; a resilient, responsible, creative and practical approach produces effective results.

My friend and mentor, Lida Melia, has left a generous legacy to many fans. Her ideas live on in this book; I hope it does justice to her brilliantly simple, yet effective approach to becoming savvy.

Read a section every day for thirty days. Mull the ideas over. Try a few on. Sometimes all it takes to work smarter is a different perspective.

Before reading further try this exercise.

Intersect and connect all nine dots by drawing four straight lines. The only restriction is, that once you begin, you cannot lift your pen off the paper.

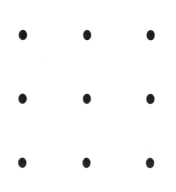

Figure. 1

Many people attempt to work the problem by drawing their four lines this way, outlining the figure, creating a box . . .

Figure. 2

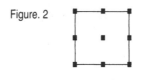

Here's one of the many different ways you can accomplish this task

Figure. 3

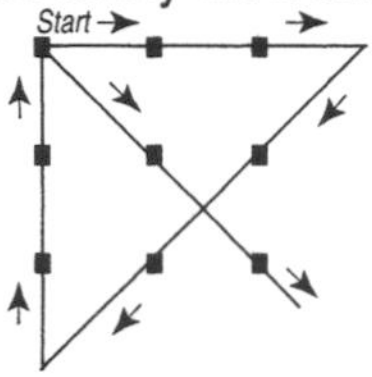

"But you didn't say I could go outside the lines!", is a typical response.

I didn't say you couldn't. The only restriction was to not pick your pen up from the paper. Any other restriction was self-imposed.

The second figure can serve to illustrate what I call "box-like thinking." When we limit ourselves to strategies that fit withing our current skillset or comfort zone, we create a box. If the behaviors inside the box work . . . keep using them. Don't fix what isn't broken.

But when the strategies we typically use don't work, we need to get "out of the box" and try different behaviors.

This different perspective may feel wrong or risky, or even rub up against your values. I do not believe it is wise to operate outside of your core value system; but just because something feels wrong . . . doesn't mean it is wrong. It just may be unfamiliar.

Note:
Throughout the book I've taken some liberty with grammatical rules . . . to reinforce an "out of the box" look. If disregarding the rules of grammar upsets you, turn to page 36.

Table of Contents

1

Savvy

Savvy is a slang word that describes a special awareness, an extraordinary grasp of what it takes to operate effectively in any given situation. Observe a savvy person and you will see an economy of effort. They work smart and maneuver gracefully. Smooth! Savvy players quickly determine the game and the rules of play.

They are alert, aware and ready to learn. Above all, they understand that every situation is unique and are therefore prepared to adapt.

While we were growing up, most of us were taught that all it should take to succeed was a willingness to work hard. Later we discovered the value of positive thinking, time management and other important self-help topics in popular books.

So we got our degrees, worked very hard and watched other people get promoted.

Many believers in the Horatio Alger model of success, "pull yourself up by your own boot straps", now feel frustrated and disillusioned with "the system". They don't want to "play games" to get ahead. So instead of figuring out what works, they stubbornly insist that their way should work.

Savvy people understand that a "game" is just someone's or some group's preferred style and behavior. Conducting business over lunch in Russia is very different than in Saudia Arabia. Buying a round of drinks in Moscow may facilitate the sale . . . and may get you escorted to the border in the Middle East.

The behavior that served me well in my home town in Minnesota, landed me in jail in Africa. At the time I lacked what I now teach . . . "system savvy".

Some people refer negatively to savvy behavior as

"political" . . . and it is. Politics is simply the ability to get other people to follow your decisions. Every effective person understands the value of influencing; in order to succeed, we need the cooperation and collaboration of others.

When someone hires you, they assume that not only can you do the work, but you have the know-how, the savvy, to get it done. Would you rather hire the best technically trained lawyer in the world, who operates naively? . . . or a good lawyer who demonstrates courtroom savvy?

Hard work and talent do pay off . . . if you invest some of that hard work in developing a talent called . . . savvy.

Elephant

How many times a day do you find that you are "right"; at work, at home, in the grocery line or at church?

The chances are you are "right" more than you know, but your being right doesn't make me or anyone else wrong.

Erik Erikson, the great psychologist, said there are 360 ways to view an elephant, when you stand at various points on a circle around the elephant. Each person on the circle sees what they see and that becomes the truth. Any other viewpoint must be wrong.

In reality, most of us only see a sliver of the truth, one part of the elephant . . . a toenail, an earlobe . . . and think we've seen the whole elephant, the whole truth. Much of the arguing and debating we indulge in over office issues, family matters or community politics is from the narrow perspective of . . . "I am right".

The boss may have denied you a raise because he has it in for you. That's true. It may also be true that he has it in for you because you are not carrying your share of the responsibility or being cooperative in areas that are important to him.

John may have been promoted because he has "buddies" in the Board Room; but John may also be perfect for the job.

It is true that hard work pays off for Bob; but not true for Kim who works in an illegal sweat shop.

Growing up in a small town in the relatively safe "50's" led me to believe the world is safe. A child of the ghetto has a different truth.

It's hard to get a handle on the truth because our sight is limited. We are almost always dealing in truth-fragments.

Imagine . . . a new employee standing at the rear of the

elephant, the boss in the front. "Tell me about this elephant, this organization," says the newcomer. "Well, it's big and gray," says the boss. "Yes," agrees the employee. "And it has a long thing which moves and sways freely", says the boss referring to the trunk. "I see it too," replies the newcomer looking at the tail. "It uses this thing to pick up food and feed itself," states the old-timer. "Fool!" says the new employee, "this animal doesn't feed itself, in fact, it does the unspeakable. You're trying to trick me!"

In the work world people have similar miscommunications. Advice backfires. What always worked for Pete may get Susan fired. What is true in sales may not work in production. In the case of the elephant, advice to "jump on the 'thing' hanging down" will get you a ride, in one case, or a "tail spin" in another.

It makes sense to "walk around the elephant", challenging your perspective getting as many views as you can. Ask others to walk with you and you will all gain wisdom from what you learn . . . and time you don't have to spend on deciding . . . who is right.

Mastering Opportunity

Opportunity is said to come but once. The person who said that probably meant once a day, an hour or even a minute. Dale Carnegie said that in every adversity lies opportunity and . . . adversity visits us more than once!

There is a story about a beggar standing on a street corner in the rain. A limousine stopped before him and the wealthy owner offered the tramp a ride to shelter. While riding together the two men asked each other questions about their lifestyles. Eventually the poor man said, "Tell me how you got so rich."

"I was always looking for opportunity," came the answer. The limousine stopped to let the beggar out. When the door opened the rich man said, "Look out for that curb! Someone ought to make cement that doesn't crumble so easily."

You can guess what happens in a story like this. The beggar went on to develop a superior cement and made his fortune.

While speaking at a conference in the Midwest, I met an inspiring woman. She was denied a chance for a sales position in an old, conservative insurance company . . . because she was a woman. No amount of hard work or persistence broke the barrier. So she left, started her own company and within a few years her company revenues topped $25 million.

Opportunity surrounds us. It's in the air we breathe. We close the door to it with thoughts like: "It won't work.", "It's been tried before.", "It's never been done.", "I'm too old . . . too young . . . too black . . . or too white."

Maybe it's a full-blown opportunity that comes but once; the kind you don't have to lift a finger to get, like winning the lottery or a grand prize drawing.

Becoming an opportunity master is like becoming the master of anything. You work at it, utilizing the "3-R's of Success"; resiliency, resourcefulness and responsible risk-taking.

The more your company or community changes, the more opportunities those changes present. The Japanese character for the word crisis, translates to "opportunity riding on a dangerous wind."

I was a delegate to the Moscow Business Conference in 1991. Moscow can be a dismal place. It is difficult to find a cup of coffee, or people who are willing to serve it to you. As a tourist I saw the lack of commonplace services and ordinary products . . . as a business woman, I saw the opportunities.

If mastering opportunity seems too hard . . . perhaps you are too soft. It is amazing how you can soften up a situation by hardening your resolve.

"Look out! . . . that curb is crumbling!"

7

Pick Battles Wisely

A sage woman, veteran of many corporate conflicts, once counseled me, "Pick your battles wisely. You have limited ammunition and you can't win them all".

Good advice! I pass it along frequently when others seek my counsel. I ask, "What's your goal? What do you gain by winning this one? What do you give up? Can you win, or is this a sacrifice play? Will winning this battle cost you the war?"

In the heat of the moment, many people sound the trumpet and charge. They don't stop to pick the time or the place. They don't scout the opponent's strengths.

This is especially critical when doing battle with a "king". . . it is lethal to merely wound a king.

When President Reagan was in office, he was scheduled to address a national womens' organization's convention. His schedule changed and his people called to apologize. They suggested reading a telegram to the audience that the President would be happy to send.

This offended the organization's leaders. They already believed Mr. Reagan didn't support women . . . so they decide to kill the king.

The women started a campaign to discredit the President. They held a news conference and placed negative advertisements in the press. Did they hurt the President? They didn't even scratch him.

They could have asked for a substitute speaker or a rain-check or for five minutes in the oval office. Wounding this king accomplished nothing important and their behavior advertised their lack of savvy.

Picking your battles wisely does not guarantee success. You will win some and lose some.

There are times when you will purposely lose a few up front. This gains you leverage for future concessions and can also cause the other side to underestimate you.

How you lose is critical to your future success. You want to be known for winning and losing well.

There are times to retreat and times to charge again. You may huddle with your own team or seek advice from those to whom you've lost. You may postpone the battle or withdraw completely.

Before you commit your time, reputation and allies . . . pick your battles wisely!

Alliances

In your personal life, you want to and need to limit access to your inner circle . . . your home, your heart. It is totally appropriate to limit your friends and loved ones to those who share your values and have your best interest at heart . . . just a few select people, ones you trust.

It is totally inappropriate, however, to limit your professional relationships, which I refer to as alliances, in the same manner. At work, pick your alliances based on who you need and not based on who you like!

Many people don't make the critical distinction between allies and friends. They believe you must have a relationship with someone before you can work with them. Nonsense!

Allies don't have to be friends. They have to be on the same side of an issue, be willing to provide assistance and agree to back and support you on that issue. You choose allies for the resources they bring . . . their experience, connections, information, equipment, skill and more.

Forming alliances with people with whom you are uncomfortable may feel wrong, hypocritical . . . like selling out.

At work you are rarely given a chance to select your co-workers. You are expected to be able to work with those whom you need to get the job done. I am amazed at how much energy is diverted from getting the job done to helping people deal with interpersonal problems. You may find friends at work, but you are wise to make allies.

Savvy players do not limit their effectiveness by choosing potential allies only from their list of likeable folk. They choose allies project by project. You may side with George on one issue and oppose him on another. These alliances may be temporary but they are always based on need.

A friend of mine, who is a staunch environmentalist, has made connections with powerful people in the oil and lumber industries. She has lunch with them in Washington and takes them on wilderness white-water raft trips. While some environmentalists accuse her of selling out, I applaud her quiet and effective influencing.

So many problems, large and small, could be effectively solved if individuals and groups would give up their righteous exclusivity and work together. Imagine what an alliance between the anti-abortion and pro-abortion groups could accomplish if they would agree to disagree on one issue and work together on another issue . . . like feeding poor children.

Young members of Los Angeles gangs are currently meeting and planning joint business ventures. If these two warring groups can sit down together so can you and the person who irritates you the most.

To be effective you need strong, powerful and useful allies. Build your professional alliances with those you need. In your personal life be as exclusive as you want in choosing your friends.

Approval

Everyone wants approval. Some people go to great lengths to get it. A few people live for it. Seeking approval can be an expensive habit costing you your peace of mind . . . or even your career.

The quest for approval begins in the cradle. We all demonstrate "political" ability very early when we discover which behaviors lead to food, love and care. Behaviors approved of by our parents result in rewards. Disapproval hurts.

When children enter school, they already understand the approval/disapproval system very well. The rewards they receive are always preceded by the approval of someone in authority.

Every savvy eight year old knows that she must determine the approved of behaviors of each teacher. Give the teacher what the teacher wants and you get what you want. By the time an individual is in graduate school she plays this game well.

This skill is useful in the beginning of your career, because pleasing the boss brings rewards.

As you move up the corporate levels the system changes. Rewards are not given out based upon getting people to like you . . . but as a result of effective decision making. The decisions made in the business world are often tough and unpopular.

The chronic approval-seeker risks becoming an ineffective yes-man. Even if he obtains approval, the hoped for rewards may not follow.

If you spend all your time, energy and skill seeking approval . . . some people will approve of you and some won't.

If you spend no time, energy or skill seeking approval, the result is the same. Use your resources to achieve your goal, and ironically, you are more likely to get the approval of those who have the rewards.

When I became a new mother some people criticized my work habits. I was in sales and my family was dependent on my income. I brought home the commissions and suffered the critics' disapproval. Seeking to please, I began to change my behaviors . . . and my sales suffered. Now different people approved and disapproved of me.

So I gave up trying to please the multitudes. I concentrated my energy on my goals and when I achieved them . . . some people approved and some didn't.

You can't please everyone. Simple, yet true!

This is not to say you should never be concerned with obtaining approval; it's a basic human need. Surround yourself with family and friends who will give you lots of approval.

But at work determine if obtaining approval is a critical factor. There may be times you are disapproved of yet still get rewarded . . . you fulfilled the need.

Simply stated, seeking approval gets you stuck . . . seeking disapproval gets you fired . . . seeking solutions gets you rewarded.

People, Paper, Radar

Corporate America is not a democracy. Access to the executive floor is severely limited and decisions affecting everyone in the organization are made in secret.

Since information that may affect your advancement and success is not published daily, it is no wonder that many savvy individuals cultivate both overt and covert sources of information . . . people, paper and radar.

Information gathering starts with people. The more broad based your network the better informed you'll be.

An established national firm once offered me a chance to start a new division that would focus on the emerging female market. The President was enthusiastic, the timing seemed right and the resources were available. I flew to headquarters, was duly courted . . . and then did a little investigative snooping.

I found someone who had been there forever and over lunch discovered that this same idea had been proposed three times before. It was a politically correct idea, but the project never had the committed backing of the necessary people to make it work. I paid for lunch and flew home.

Information is a traded commodity. To get some you have to give some . . . beyond water cooler gossip. Information that people need to know to make appropriate decisions is the currency. Honor confidentiality, however. To be known as a "sieve" is not savvy!

Another way to keep informed is by paper. Read everything

about your company, it's product and it's competition. Annual reports, press releases, trade publications, speeches and internal memos reveal vital information. Learn to read between-the-lines. Decipher your company's code. What does "Harry left to spend more time with his family" really mean?

Finally, develop radar . . . notice things. Who used to be available and now isn't ? Who, suddenly, is everywhere? Who did or did not get invited to what?

New buzz-words can signal new directions. For years while conducting seminars at a large company, I heard the managers talk about creativity and innovation. Within the span of a few months, the words profit and revenue were all I heard . . . a fairly obvious clue that the game had changed.

Notice where money is being spent, where cut backs are happening, who or what is in favor and who or what is on the way out.

This intelligence gathering requires time, energy, and a willingness to look-up from your desk, come in early, have lunch in the break room, drop in for a chat with people from different departments and tune into the grapevine. A few extra minutes a day gathering intelligence will better prepare you for the job you are paid to accomplish.

Knowledge is power.

Politics

"I'm not surprised at Harry's promotion. He's a masterful politician", said Joe. "Yes", responded his teammate, "the same happened with Ruth . . . ten years at the telephone company and now she's in senior management. She plays the game well!"

Are they describing business people or politicians? . . . Both!

Some people think that politicians just run for office and "divvy" up the tax dollars. Others believe that politics has no place in the office. And many people judge politics as bad, distasteful and negative . . . and can't define it beyond that.

Actually, political ability is the single most important attribute of any business or social leader. There are good and bad politics. When politics are missing, altogether, chaos reigns. Politics, very simply put, is the ability to get other people to follow your decisions. There are over 50 different ways to get other people to follow you; inexperienced or ineffective people limit themselves to six.

A favorite political maneuver of some powerful people is persuasion, proving one way or another that their suggestions are superior, that they are "right" or that their ideas are the best. Powerful persuaders are successful in getting others to follow.

But the rest of us, usually, have to offer something-in-return to be persuasive. We may have to offer money, corporate benefits, opportunity or recognition. People who are successful in business and in their communities have learned to barter to get what they want. "You give me what I want and in return I give you what you want", has been the political basis for business since the cave-dwelling days.

Threats are another popular persuasion strategy; however,

threat only works with insecure and easily intimidated employees. Timid, meek and weak workers cannot keep a company successful for long. So if threatening your employees works for you, you have a bigger problem than you realize.

Whatever your position at work . . . "Grand Poobah", "New Kid on the Block", "Low Man on the Totem Pole" . . . your effectiveness is greatly enhanced by honing your political skills to get those around you to follow your lead.

Who's Your Customer?

Who's your customer? No, not your company's customer, your customer? To whom do you sell your skills and talents?

Your company! Well . . . what kind of customer service are you giving?

Just as your company has a greater awareness that its customers have more options in this competitive environment, you also need to be aware that you face increasing competition.

This year IBM announced a lay-off to 20,000 astonished workers who believed it would never happen to them. These people joined the ranks of thousands of others in search of a new "customer" . . . the next employer.

Many of you want and expect the company to take care of you. Please! Reverse your thinking for your own protection! Take care of your customer, the one who signs your check, because in the long run the customer is . . . the boss.

Consider adapting the following good service techniques:

1. An Appreciative Attitude. Smile, say thanks. Demonstrate a willingness to be of service that says, "I'm happy to be here, eager to work."

2. Go The Extra Mile. Instead of saying "It's not my job!" try saying . . . "I'll get it done for you." In a large company, one department communicated their willingness to be of service by adopting the motto . . . "We do windows". Not

only did they place the motto on their walls but they followed through with the type of service that got noticed upstairs.

3. The Customer is Always Right. Now don't be silly here! I don't mean that you can't present a different point of view or offer options . . . that demonstrates a willingness to satisfy your customer.

4. Know the Customer. Do your homework. Make sure you know the company's mission, its products, the challenges it faces and the goals for the future.

5. Offer Solutions. No customer buys your product, they buy the benefit. Anticipate the needs of your company and be proactive with solutions.

6. Respect Your Customer. Do not bad mouth your company. Do not bad mouth your boss.

Give good service! Does it always pay off? No . . . but I can't imagine bad service ever does.

Uniforms

Have you ever noticed that men always wear uniforms?

A common assumption is that women spend more time thinking about clothing than men. Not true.

It's just that men and women use clothes to make very different "political" statements.

When men get together, in an organized activity, they create and wear uniforms. We see it in sports but you can also observe it at work.

Is there a uniform for bank officials? For computer engineers? For eccentric professors? Yes, there is! Would a construction worker wear a pink shirt? At home maybe, but probably not on the site.

Men pick clothing that helps them say, "I'm on the team.", "I belong here.", and "Notice my rank." Items like Italian leather shoes, a Rolex watch, school ties and handmade shirts further point out the status of the member.

Remember General Schwartzkopf's televised appearances? He always wore his khakis ("I'm on the team."); but you immediately noticed the stars on his lapel ("This is my rank.").

The man dressed in a shirt and tie, on a construction site, is most likely in a position of authority.

We women tend to make a different political statement with our clothing. Why did we strongly reject the "dress for success" look of the early "80's"? While the idea of a feminine corporate uniform made sense, the "navy blue suit, bow tie and low pump" look was around for a brief time only.

We can't stand to look alike. Our clothing is used to distinguish us one from another. It says, "Look at me, I'm unique".

Imagine five women at a gathering all wearing the same outfit. How would they respond? . . . They'd be horrified!

I was at an important cocktail reception wearing my new houndstooth check jacket, flecked with rhinestones. Then I noticed her . . . another woman in the same jacket! We successfully avoided each other for the first thirty minutes. But when our escorts began to talk to each other we did too. We both exclaimed, "Oh, look at us, can you believe it?"; all the while, eying each other to see who looked better.

Now imagine five men at a gathering, all are wearing similar blue suits, white shirts and red-striped ties. How would they respond? Silently, with sighs of relief . . . "Thank God I dressed right!"

Why do men and women respond so differently in similar situations? My theory? The male culture is more team oriented. Men have more history, experience, tradition and success being aligned with each other. The female culture traditionally emphasized the value of being unique, being noticed, and being chosen . . . by men.

Ladies, we don't need to borrow men's clothing, but it would do us wonders to borrow their powerful, effective strategy of teamplay.

Resumes

What is the first thing people do when they're looking for work?

Write a resume!

But when you think about it, resumes aren't necessarily the most important tool for getting work or the good job. In fact, they can be detrimental.

You write a resume because you want something different. You are unemployed and want a job or you are employed and want to work for someone else. In either case, you want to change your circumstances.

On most resumes, individuals describe what they are doing now or did on their previous job; they write about what they no longer want to do.

One client asked me to help him get a job in advertising. It was a new field for him; but he believed his copywriting and promotional skills were sufficient to gain him entry. I looked at his resume. What I saw astounded me! He had described his 17 years of experience in teaching, not the talents that would land him a new career. Teaching was the field he wanted to leave . . . the position he no longer wanted.

So, we tore up the resume, created a portfolio to demonstrate his skills in advertising, sent a clever introductory circular to key advertising people and obtained free speaking engagements for him to share his advertising know-how. He loves his new job.

Martha was a homemaker who had raised six kids, shepherded her husband's career to executive status and was an active volunteer for many community organizations. After her spouse died she obtained a degree and sought work as a manager.

Management, after all, was what she knew. She also knew that scouting events and "save the whale" campaigns could be seen a detriment, not an asset, to getting the job she desired.

So she made a list of key people; business leaders and owners she had met over the years and scheduled interviews with them. A prominent bank president started their interview with, "Martha, tell me about yourself".

Martha's creative reply was, "Yes, thank you, I will, but if you don't mind I'd like to talk about the job first." With his permission she presented the facts and figures she had researched about his organization; gave her outsider's perspective on potential problems and issues; proposed a plan for improvements; and, finally, offered him a no-risk trial period for her services. Martha was hired and quickly rose to senior management.

The problem with resumes is they focus the attention on you. No company hires you because they like you or because your resume is well written.

They hire you because they have a need. Demonstrating your ability to fulfill their need, not typesetting . . . gets you hired.

Meta-Communication

Communication is a complicated process. What you say and how you say it is only a small part of the actual message. You know what you are saying. Do you know what you are communicating?

Meta-communication is the message that gets communicated . . . often not the message that was intended.

One of my college professors was always encouraging us to drop by his office whenever we needed help. He said he was "there for us". When I dropped by his office, I noticed only one chair, and he was sitting in it. What did . . . no place to sit, say?

My former bank has a very prominently displayed slogan: "We care more about you than your money". Frequently the tellers' and loan officers' actions spoke louder than the slogan. I changed banks.

People always "get" meta-communication, whether it's consciously or sub-consciously.

You can't put your finger on why you don't trust Marge; but you don't. She could be undeserving of trust or she is meta-communicating something she doesn't intend by many small inconsistent behaviors.

You claim you are a team player. But when your boss was reassuring his boss that the project would be completed on time, you interrupted and said that the project was dangerously behind schedule. What got communicated to either boss?

You ask the people in your organization to be risk-takers;

but, when they take a risk and fail, you sharply criticize them.

You are an Hispanic woman and valuing diversity is one of your causes; but you automatically dismiss any idea or plan proposed by a white male.

"We value our employees", is a company's motto; however, close, safe and convenient parking is reserved for senior management only.

"We are a Total Quality Company ", declares the owner while asking his people to ship slightly defective products.

Their behaviors don't support their intended message.

Aware or unaware, we are always communicating! Speaking up or remaining silent communicates. Attending the meeting or skipping the meeting communicates.

Analyze your behavior. Is it consistent with your desired message? Do you "walk your talk"? Your intention doesn't count . . .what you meta-communicate does!

Make Your Boss Look Good

Your "#1" job as an employee is to make your boss "look good".

This sentence will cause some of you to throw this book in the trash. I can hear the protests now . . . "But my boss is a jerk!" . . . "He does nothing!" . . ." We all cover for her!" . . . "My boss is totally incompetent!"

You are hired to help the organization succeed. I have met so many employees who do not understand this very basic organizational fact of life. You are required to do your job as well as help others do theirs.

That means taking a share of the work from the secretaries when they are overwhelmed. It means helping a cohort when they are stuck on a technical problem. And it means, it especially means . . . making the boss look good.

In the business world we are all dependent upon each others' talents and skills. It is in your own best interest to fortify, cover for, support and carry those people who are involved in the same work.

Still don't buy it?

Well, let's say you are correct, your boss is incompetent. And you tell everyone, over and over again. Then you sit back, watch your boss dig the hole deeper and wait for her to fall in. Now . . . who's watching your behavior? Not only your boss, but your boss's boss!

Let's say that you play differently. You not only cover for your boss or your teammates, but you actually go in and help them do their work better. Now . . . who's watching? Your boss and all the other bosses.

Who would you rather have on your team; someone who points out your inadequacies or someone who pitches in to ensure your success?

It's in your own self-interest to help those above you and around you.

I know some employees who would rather die than make their boss look good . . . and they will. Cutting your boss down in public is political suicide. It tells every other boss in your company that you are not a team player but a disloyal troublemaker, who can and will sabotage the best efforts of the group.

To belittle or disparage your boss among your peers is like chopping a hole in the bottom of the boat just because you don't like the skipper. When you are successful in scuttling the boat, you will most likely be kicked off the life raft.

Your career depends upon the successful project in which you have been involved; not just your individual talents. Your record needs to reflect your ability to work effectively with others.

So roll up your sleeves . . . quit rolling your eyes . . . and demonstrate your ability to be a team player. Go ahead! Make your boss look good!

The Glass Ceiling

Much has been said and written about the "glass ceiling". Studies prove it exists. Many of us have experienced it first hand. It's real.

It is defined as the invisible barrier that keeps women and minorities from reaching the highest levels in organizations.

Fear, prejudice and resistance to change are obvious reasons for the barrier. There is an additional subtle factor.

It is comfort. By the time people are in position for a job on the top floor, competency is no longer an issue. Everyone is qualified. The invitations are usually handed out to the people with whom "they" are comfortable; not all white men get invited either.

Decisions made at the top are difficult ones. The fate of the company and all its' people are in their hands. The debates are often bloody. There are turf battles, ego showdowns and continual negotiation for resources.

The top floor is stressful under ordinary circumstances. The addition of a person or people who are different increases the stress.

At the top they need to be able to openly debate, "no holds-barred"; but with someone who is different they often feel like they are walking on eggshells. Will they offend? Will they be accused of sexism or racism? Will they get sued? These possibilities hinder the development of relationships necessary in the inner circle. This hurts productivity.

Being uncomfortable is not a justifiable excuse for maintaining the glass ceiling, but it is a factor.

So what do you do if you'd like to remove this invisible but very real barrier?

If you're on the top floor, you need to get comfortable with being uncomfortable. You need to get experience with people on the lower floors to form good working relationships; relationships that can handle honest communication and a good debate or two.

If you want to be invited upstairs you need to allow them to get more comfortable with you. That means dropping the protective shield you may have developed. Can you handle criticism? Do you own your mistakes? Do you offer solutions? Can you depersonalize in emotionally tense situations? Can you become part of the team . . . or do you use your difference to stand apart?

The glass ceiling is preventing good business. We desperately need the cream, the best ideas and talents, to rise to the top of our organizations. People upstairs and downstairs must work together, comfortably . . . and uncomfortably, to shatter this Berlin Wall of business.

Power

There is nothing really mysterious about power. It is simply the ability to make a decision that other people decide to follow. When other people decide to follow your decisions you have power.

The baby who can get his parents to feed him in the middle of the night has power. The young professional who can get her boss to adopt her suggestion has power. We assume Presidents of the United States always have power, but Presidents who cannot get Congress to confirm their budgets lack power, in that instance.

It is a common error to assume that titles and positions confer power; in fact it is the other way around.

Most executives and other officials made decisions and got others to follow them before they were promoted into positions of authority. Just as the limousine comes after you create your wealth, the positions of responsibility come after you create and demonstrate your power.

No one can give another person power. If the boss puts you in charge during his absence and tells your co-workers to follow you, you may think you have power. In reality, no one is following you, they are following the boss's decision to follow you.

Those who enjoy power are dependent upon those who decide to follow their decisions. Even the most feared dictator must have people following his decisions if he is to keep his power. When the people of Romania were willing to follow Premier Ceausescu, he had power. The day the people and his army decided to withdraw their support was the end of his tyranny. If his army had continued to side with him he would still be in charge, but the army's decision, to no longer follow Ceausescu's decisions left him eternally unempowered.

If you aspire to leadership, you must first be able to make decisions. This requires vision and courage because for the decision-maker there are no answers "in the back of the book."

Then you must get others to follow you . . . persuade, negotiate, sell your idea, offer carrots or threaten sticks. There are over 50 different ways to get others to follow your decisions. You need to know them all!

Finally, take care of those who empower you. Share your vision with them, solicit their advice, listen to their critiques and be sure to say thanks . . . . because there is no such person as a "self-made man" who did it all alone.

"Power . . . The ability to make decisions that other people decide to follow."

Win Win

It is chic today to talk about win/win negotiations, resolutions or compromises as if win/win was a new concept. In fact, the win/win approach has been around as long as people have been conducting business.

The problem is that today, people are implying win/win means "equal-equal" and "fair-fair".

Sal thinks he is engaging in win/win behavior when he gives paid holidays to his employees after they take his required polygraph tests. To Sal this is win/win all the way. He wins by having a controllable workforce; the employees win with paid vacation time.

The problem is that most employees object to polygraphs with or without time off. Is this win/win?

Liz thinks she is engaging in win/win when she sells a hard-to-move car at a rock-bottom price. The customer preferred another style with more amenities but couldn't resist the major price reduction.

Both parties have compromised by giving up something they really wanted; one a large commission check and the other air conditioning. They may think they are getting a bargain today, but when Liz loses the salesperson of the month bonus and the customer swelters in the August heat, neither will be pleased with the deal.

Win /win may involve concessions and compromises on both sides. One side does not get to decide what is fair for both; nor does win/win mean that both sides have to be equally inconvenienced or disappointed.

Bob and Fred are negotiating the price of a trash removal contract. Bob fights hard for his company suggesting concession after concession and asking for more than the standard services. Fred stands his ground on many issues and insists on getting top dollar.

Both gentlemen drive the negotiation hard and take whatever they can get. After two hours, they sign the contract, pleased with their respective deals. In other words, both think they "won" the negotiation.

This is win/win in its truest form. Each person negotiates the best deal possible for himself and acknowledges the same rights for the other side.

Win/win is not always 50/50. Mary might negotiate 90% and concede you 10%. Equally competent people may negotiate unequal results; but If they both think they have won . . . they have.

Take Care Of You

Many of us were taught to believe that if we were good, obeyed the rules and did what we were told, we would get what we wanted . . . we would get taken care of.

That may have been true when we were children; but as adults, it is our job to take care of ourselves.

We often try to take care of ourselves, by taking care of others . . . hoping . . . they'll take care of us. This round-about behavior usually leaves us feeling disappointed, used or taken for granted when the people we have taken care of don't respond in the way we expect.

Fred really appreciated that Marge went the "extra mile" for him at work. He said, "Marge, I owe you one!" She replied, "Oh, no, not really Fred . . . it was nothing. I was happy to do it."

Two weeks later she asked Fred for a small favor. Fred said he was going to play golf and couldn't do it. Again, she graciously replied, "I understand" . . . but walked away feeling that Fred had taken advantage of her.

Now wait a minute! Earlier Fred acknowledged his appreciation and willingness to repay Marge. She said "no, it was nothing!" She was playing the game of "let's pretend you don't owe me but read my mind and figure out that you do".

There are many people like Marge that are uncomfortable taking care of themselves. They find it difficult to say, "Of course you owe me Fred, but I'm sure you'll be there for me when I need a favor" . . . and then reminding Fred if need be.

The Marge's of the world attempt to take care of themselves . . . by taking care of others.

Marge needs to learn what the airline attendant teaches us each time we fly . . . "put your own oxygen mask on before assisting others."

Taking care of yourself does not automatically mean short changing others. Relationships work best when they are mutually beneficial. It makes good sense to help others get what they want.

It's OK to ask yourself, "What's in this for me?" or "How do I get the best deal I can?" It is only when you are confident and comfortable with the deal you just cut for yourself that you are capable and willing to allow the other side their win.

Whose job is it to take care of you? . . . yours!

Rules Are Guidelines

Why do we have rules, policies and regulations? "To control us" is a typical response.

While rules can be and are used for that purpose, rules are best used as guidelines to help us reach goals. If the rule moves us closer to the goal, obey it.

But when the rules become the obstacle we need to consider bending, breaking or ignoring them . . . going beyond the rules, making new ones.

For example, our society desires safe traffic flow on our streets. We erect stop signs and make a rule to stop at them. To the extent that stopping at the sign achieves safety, we need to stop!

But, what if there was a two-ton truck behind you and the driver leans out the window and yells, "I have no brakes!" Would you stop at the sign? . . . of course not! Stopping at this sign, obeying this rule, will cause an accident and may get you a traffic violation.

Many people in organizations, seeking to do the right thing, get the list of rules and obey them implicitly . . . unaware of the risk in doing so.

Is it risky to disobey the rules? You bet!

But blindly following the rule book is also risky!

When I hired a new office administrator I told her my negotiating policies, expecting them to be followed. I also said, if you follow these policies precisely . . . and blow a million dollar opportunity, I'll help you find a new job."

You see, we are really paid to think, to make decisions, to reach goals. Keep your eye on the desired outcome, not the policy.

While presenting these ideas at a company sponsored seminar, the owner, in back of the room, raised his hand. I had just told his people to disobey rules and wondered if he was objecting.

He said, "Let me pass on some advice I was given, early in my career. You are of no use to the organization if you disobey all the rules . . . nor if you obey all the rules. It is the somewhere-in-between that increases your value."

Now, where do you find the magic book that tells you exactly when to obey and when to disregard? There isn't one! Savvy players understand that every situation requires a custom tailored strategy.

We know that breaking the rules is risky. That lesson was learned early. But many opportunities have been lost by mere obstacles disguised as rules. Remember, there are only ten rules written in stone!

So keep your eye on the goal . . . and out of the rule book.

Connections

People who work smart understand the value of developing connections. Having access to the right people brings access to information, advice, resources . . . and protection.

Developing connections that help you work effectively requires an investment of time, energy and resources.

Some people are blessed with powerful family or school connections. Others develop useful connections through community service, professional organizations, special task forces and even hobbies.

I often hear people complaining that they would like to have a drink with the guys, play golf, volunteer or join that club say . . . "but I don't have enough time", . . . "I have three kids at home" or . . . "I leave my work at the office".

We all have unique situations that make finding the time or committing our energies difficult. But understand there is a price you pay for not making the effort and taking the time to develop useful connections.

Doris was a single parent, supporting her family by selling houses in the $100,000 price range. She knew it took the same time, effort and energy to sell a $600,000 house as it did to sell a $100,000 house . . . but she didn't know $600,000 buyers.

However she did know someone who was a member of an exclusive yacht club in her town. She asked that person to introduce her to a single man; she didn't care if he was young, old, divorced or gay . . . just single.

So her friend introduced her to an elegant, elderly gentleman. She explained to the gentleman that she'd like to be escorted once a month to a yacht club event. There she would have the chance to meet people who bought expensive homes. The gentleman was an eccentric writer who could use her organizational and typing skills. So she typed and he escorted. Within one year she was selling $600,000 houses!

She bartered her skills for access to new connections, demonstrating another characteristic of savvy people . . . they play a mutually beneficial game.

Invest some time and effort developing connections with people who have resources you need or might need. At the same time, learn to value and leverage your own resources, so that you position yourself as . . . someone who is useful to know.

Systems

Whenever anyone says to me that she doesn't want to play games at work, she just wants to be herself . . . I have to ask which behaviors reveal "the real you", cheering at a football game or crying at a funeral?"

The person who says they don't want to play politics in the office is really making an extraordinary statement. He is demanding that everyone pay attention to his comfort and accommodate his desires, without returning the favor. He wants everyone to play "his game".

In the real world, people must accommodate each other to earn cooperation, support and respect. The trick is that this is accomplished differently in each culture and organization.

Every group establishes it's own procedures, guidelines and taboos. Working for the government is different than working for an airline; and working at TWA is different than working at United.

The savvy individual learns how to read each system and act accordingly. What works . . . works!

Paul has always been rewarded for his superior technical skills; but his new job in a small start-up company requires additional abilities. The company needs him to be more market oriented and customer focused. Paul must adapt.

Bob's been around for a long time. He and his former boss played golf together and were in the same Rotary club. Marilyn, his new boss, has a "bee in her bonnet" for any perceived old boys system. Bob must adapt some of his behaviors to meet her cultural needs.

Well . . . what if you have to adapt too much? Should you still play the game? Probably not for the long haul; but it doesn't hurt to demonstrate your flexibility and savvy while you are looking for or creating a better situation.

As the pace of change increases in organizations, "system savvy" becomes a more frequently used tool from your professional toolbox.

"What's the game?" "How do I play?" "Which game do I choose to play?"

Ask yourself these questions often. It will serve you better than declaring . . . "I don't play games at work."

Establish Motive

Goals, Goals, Goals . . . company goals, team goals and your own goals. You need to set them, achieve them and help others reach theirs.

Savvy individuals do one better. They determine the motive or the purpose behind the goal.

The President of a long established and respected small manufacturing company contacted me when he took over running the family business. He wanted me to help him find Total Quality Management (TQM) training programs.

Before suggesting an obvious strategy, recommending a colleague, I took the time to chat with this fellow. During our lengthy yet casual conversation his motive was revealed.

He wanted his "numbers" to beat his brother's. Aha! The motive behind the new emphasis on quality was sibling rivalry.

Knowing why a goal is set is basic to determining the strategy!

Understanding the underlying motive helps protect you from potential traps in people's stated goals.

Let's say I took this President's goal at face value and helped implement a TQM program . . . but the ensuing changes brought a drop in quarterly profits.

By achieving the goal, providing TQM training . . . I would have failed! When all was said and done, increasing the numbers was the real goal.

Police detectives always try to determine motive. It helps

point them in the right direction. Establishing motive can keep you from taking a wrong turn.

Your company might be encouraging innovation. But your boss may be retiring soon, he doesn't want to rock-the-boat, so he drags his feet slowing you down. Understanding his motive may help you design plans allowing for your progress as well as offering him some protection.

Establishing motive requires detective work . . . watching, looking, listening, asking questions, reviewing history and paying attention to patterns.

Energy spent discovering motive is well worth the effort.

Achieving stated goals, without addressing the needs behind the motive, is risky. In succeeding . . . you may fail.

Basic Team Play

Everyone seems to agree that team play is required for organizational success. But not every one agrees on what constitutes good team play.

For the last ten years many companies have invested in team building sessions and exercises. Some stress interpersonal skills and creative thinking while others urge leadership to be shared and consensus achieved. Models from Japan and Germany were studied and copied.

The result? . . . People trying to be team players only to have others accuse them of not being team players!

The new team models offer a variety of creative behaviors from which to choose. Once an effective team agrees upon the goal, they also agree to follow, consciously or subconsciously, these unwritten rules.

1. OBEY THE COACH. Discussion and /or dissent may be encouraged, but the team understands those conversations are conducted "behind closed doors". When the coach outlines the game plan, a good team player responds with an, "Aye, aye Sir ". . . trusting the coach's vision, information and leadership.

2. NEVER TACKLE YOUR OWN TEAM MEMBERS . . . in public. Team players don't denigrate the team, company or leaders to outsiders. They resolve conflicts internally. They understand that they don't have to be friends to support and work effectively with each other.

3. SET ASIDE PERSONAL GOALS. Susan values visibility and would love to present the idea to the board. She knows Tom has a better shot at getting their approval. So Susan sublimates her goal to the team goal. In return, the team will find another situation for Susan to obtain visibility.

4. KNOW YOUR ROLE AND STAY IN IT. A good team doesn't act spontaneously. They have a meeting before the meeting where they brainstorm, strategize, develop contingency plans and assign roles. Bob will present the idea, Fran will bring up and shoot down the predictable objections, Hank will cheerlead, and if the client hates it . . . George will act as scapegoat. Team players understand the value of an occasional sacrifice play.

The primary purpose of forming a team is to achieve an agreed upon goal. Team building exercises and retreats can be fun and help the individuals bond. But when it's game time . . . an effective team plays by the rules.

The Power Of Payback

Have you ever noticed that busy important people organize their life to allow time to help others? I'm not referring to charity here, but rather a dynamic of power that savvy people understand . . . offering favors is a good investment.

Because other savvy players pay back!

It is simply understood, not even talked about, that when you have benefited from someone . . . you are in their debt and you owe!

You see, among equals or peers, it is expected that everyone plays a mutually beneficial game; the "I help you, you help me" game. It is the glue that binds professional relationships. It is the essence of business.

And while the game can be played with charm, grace and humor . . . it is a serious game. People do keep score.

Two people desiring to start their own consulting company asked me for advice. I agreed to meet them at a coffee shop across town. After giving them an hour of my time, sharing my wisdom and insights gathered from over 10 years of consulting experience, I got up to leave. Before I could go, they quickly looked at the bill and said "Oh, Billi, you owe 85 cents for your iced tea!"

"Sit down!", I said. "If you don't understand that you pay for my iced tea, the last hour of consulting and information will do you no good."

The shocked look on their faces revealed they didn't get it!

They just thought I was something that rhymed with rich. What they had just demonstrated was an amazingly naive approach to life. They were going to start a business without the most basic understanding of business . . . business is an exchange based on mutual benefit.

Eighty-five cents wasn't the issue; I could pay for my own iced tea. By asking me to pay, they communicated that they did not understand the give and take of business.

I didn't agree to help them because I had some specific payback in mind, nor did I see them as charity. I saw them as players and sharing advice is a good way of increasing your network. But they expected someone to give them something for free. My mistake . . . they weren't players.

People who feel empowered and equal ask for help, services or resources . . . with the expectation of paying back.

Demonstrate this savvy behavior often. Return favors! And arrange your life to have some time and resources allocated to helping others. In addition to feeling good . . . It's a good investment.

Good Ol' Boys

Let's suppose you've been given $50 million for the job of putting together a new company! Your plans require that you hire thirty key people. Where would you start? Who would you choose first?

If you are like most of the people to whom we pose this question, your answer is that you would hire the good people you know. This might add up to ten superb individuals. You still have twenty jobs left. Who would you hire next?

You most likely will hire the people they know. The five remaining positions are the ones you will offer to strangers. You see, all of us, if we get the chance, try to create our own network . . . of "ol' boys" or "ol' girls", as the case may be.

There are good reasons we act this way. Critical positions in business aren't just held by people who are technically competent. The success of the business depends upon and demands individuals who are savvy, loyal, risk-taking and reliable. These are attributes that are not discernable on resumes. Nevertheless, if your key people don't have them, you won't have a business for long.

That's why important jobs rarely go to outsiders. If the powers that be don't know enough people with the right qualifications, they will seek them through their associates.

This is not just a game for the ol' boys to play.

I was once persuaded to start and to open a restaurant in only a month. I had to scramble! Who did I hire? Everyone and anyone I had worked with in other restaurants who were good . . . and available. When I looked up one day I noticed that the crew was entirely female. A veritable ol' girls network!

Some people think that in the ol' boys network friendship is more important than skill. That's rarely the case. Just as you would not knowingly climb into a plane piloted by a very drunk friend, corporate leaders do not turn over the running of their organizations to incompetents.

It is true, however, that an executive may willingly work with an associate who has only one or two of the critical qualities of leadership. That is still preferable to working with an unknown person.

In our society who you know is a fact of life.

Are you having trouble breaking into an ol' boys network? Try demonstrating the qualities they value. Although you are an outsider, play like an insider.

Still can't get in? Start your own! I recently suggested this to a convention audience of visually impaired people, five hundred talented and ready-to-work-hard people. They've already built a national and international support organization that could easily be turned into a powerful ol' boys/girls network. "Start your own businesses," I said. "Have the folks who can see work for you!"

Who you know and who knows you counts! Your network determines your opportunities.

Power Colors

Image consultants, who advise us to "dress for success", tell us that power colors are black, navy, steel grey and red.

I believe pink can be a power color . . . if it gets you what you want.

There are numerous books and courses promoting power dressing, power gestures and even power lunching. These gurus imply there is a guaranteed path to success when you follow their "10 steps".

What truly successful and powerful people understand is that a power strategy is the one that works. What works with Sam on Tuesday, works with Sam on Tuesday. The same strategy may backfire when tried with Marge on Wednesday.

People who believe in the ten magic steps or the four guaranteed methods are living in the world of "should". Things should work . . . in a perfect world. But they don't always, that's why there's a new success manual published every week.

 We don't dwell in the land of "should" but live in the land of "what is".

Your new power suit, your redesigned resume, rehearsed interview, impressive references and totally correct posture should impress the interviewer. But she is an insecure person who doesn't own a power suit, resents your connections, is suspicious of slick resumes and finds your posture arrogant.

With a little homework, you could have worn your second best suit, reflected the interviewer's style in your speech and posture and stated your belief that background and connections aren't as important as a willingness to learn from those already on the job.

A great example of professional dress was shared by a Drug Enforcement Agency undercover agent. While busting a drug operation with three male partners she wore an ultra-feminine, big skirted, dress with bows, had her hair in curlers and wore army boots. The sight of such a person, holding a shotgun and kicking in the door, was so incongruous, it gave her partners a few extra seconds to get into position while the bad guys were still trying to make sense of what they saw.

That's a power suit!

Yes You Can!

Sarah bought a car for $13,500. The sticker price was $18,000. She's a good negotiator. So why is she quitting her job when the boss says she can't have a promotion?

It's surprising how well some people can negotiate in some circumstances but not in others.

Charlie is an independent distributor of office equipment for a major company. His products also have a "sticker price" but Charlie makes all kinds of deals.

Charlie, like Sarah, knows how to negotiate. Yet resentfully, he is paying an outrageous IRS tax bill.

"When I joined this company," Sarah says, "the recruiter told me I was qualified to work in only one department. I took the entry level position hoping I would be trained for something better. It's never happened. I can't get ahead here."

Why is it that these two intelligent people, both with good negotiating skills, play well in one situation and don't play at all in another?

The reason is simple yet subtle. Sarah and Charlie negotiate well when they feel they have been given permission. Without permission they resort to a powerless position.

Sarah knows, when she enters the automobile showroom, that the sticker price is only "pretend". Negotiation is one of the rules in the car buying game.

Charlie has been given both permission and encouragement from his company to negotiate. But at tax time, Charlie assumes the IRS game doesn't include negotiation. "Pay or go to jail is their rule", he says, and so he obeys.

Both these people misunderstand the use and power of negotiation. Negotiation is an alternative to blindly obeying the rules made up by someone else.

Every situation, every single one, is negotiable; however, it is also true that not every person negotiates.

The recruiter at Sarah's company has an obligation to hire the best people. Rarely are the best employees obedient robots without minds or voices. When Sarah opens a negotiation, she is demonstrating a sophisticated business skill which increases her potential value to the company.

The IRS does indeed carry a big stick, but negotiation is possible. If one agent won't play, ask for another one.

Our culture has a "price tag" mentality compared to other cultures where bartering and trading is a way of life. Don't let this stop you! Don't wait for permission . . . it's not needed.

View the world as one big negotiation table and cut your best deal.

53

Work Isn't Family

It seems that every organization in this country is becoming more impersonal. I hear from disgruntled employees, over and over again . . . "This company sure has changed . . . it used to be a family!"

Has the company ever really been a family? I don't think so.

A family's mission is to take care of people. The company's mission is to take care of the company.

One of the ways a company does this is to take care of it's human resources; which is different than treating them like family. A successful company will train, motivate, compensate and provide a safe work environment. This helps people work more productively.

But the company doesn't exist to take care of people by providing job security, solving their personal problems or guaranteeing a comfortable retirement. These are benefits a company can provide . . . if it is profitable.

In a very real way, helping the company succeed is the only way to job security. Still no guarantees; even valued employees are let go in times of change.

But if you demonstrate a history of being a problem-solver, an innovator and a team player you are worth more in the job market.

So for your own security develop this perspective . . . your company is not your family! The company may refer to itself as such . . . like a major company recently did in a full-page

Newsweek advertisement. But a company is not and cannot be a family!

A family doesn't put economic considerations first. You don't retire grandma when her medical expenses sky-rocket or lay-off Uncle Bob when you cut the family budget.

A family survives a bankruptcy. It doesn't have a product to market and sell. The family's job is to take care of people. The world would be a sad place if families tried to act like companies.

Companies cannot act like families. Read between-the-lines when companies call themselves a family. Don't assume they will take care of you. That is your job.

How do you take care of yourself? . . . take care of the company. Keep yourself current and your skills up to date. Think about what the company needs today and in the immediate future.

And take care of your family! When the work world disappoints you, lets you down, treats you unfairly . . . it is wonderful to have a family take care of you.

55

Leave

I frequently meet people who are eager to tell me what's wrong with their boss, their company and their co-workers. According to them the other people have the wrong goals, behave inexcusably and just won't listen.

I nod, listen, ask a few questions . . . then nod and listen again . . . and then ask . . . "Why don't you leave????"

The shocked expressions revealed their expectation that the world should change to accommodate them. Wouldn't that be wonderful?!?!

Now , I'm not talking about the "chronic complainers", those folks whose lifes' mission it is to criticize.

I'm describing a far too typical person who is unsatisfied with their present work environment. They don't agree with the goal or the plan to achieve it, are unhappy with their job description and don't back their co-workers. In short . . . the job's not a fit.

Why stay?

We scoff at people who wear unbearably painful shoes just because they were on sale or in fashion. Yet many people are in jobs that pinch them on all sides. Walking on painful feet is one thing . . . but why suffer a painful job?

Some situations you have to put up with . . . grin and bear it. But many of us have choices we don't exercise. We could up-date that resume, shop around, market ourselves better, get new skills or polish up old ones, start a business or get rid of a business.

Savvy people determine which game they want to play and how to play it. They figure out the games other people play and decide if they want to participate. They know when to "hold 'em" and when to "fold 'em".

What keeps people in the wrong jobs?

#1. Not accepting the responsibility for creating their life and sculpting it to their specifications.

#2. Fear. Believing that there is nothing better . . . nothing else available . . . that they are too old or too young . . . or, or, or . . . You've heard the litany.

So do what you can to tailor your job, adjusting it and you for a better fit. But if the job or the people rub you wrong, causing a blister . . . give it away! Leave . . . get yourself a custom-made, designed for you, opportunity.

Build Your Organization

For years success literature has encouraged you to find yourself a mentor; a powerful, experienced, organizational guru. Someone to guide you through the corporate maze, point out the pitfalls, protect you from adversaries and share wisdom earned the hard way.

It is indeed wonderful to have such an ally.

But realistically, you need a whole organization to guide, inform and protect you. An organization of people with diverse talents, rank and connections to increase your effectiveness.

While it is obvious to look up the organization for a mentor, it is also wise to look down . . . and connect with all the people you need. People below you can also make or break you.

There is a reason why people above you take their precious time and share their valuable insights. They recognize the value of building an organization.

So Lesson #1 to learn from a mentor is . . . to mentor!

A mentor is not a personal sugar daddy or fairy godmother. Although rarely discussed between the players, a mentor/mentee relationship is an alliance based on mutual benefit. You each exchange information, connections, cooperation and protection.

The mentor shares information from her perspective and position . . . so does the mentee. Information can be blocked going up the organization as well as coming down.

Some people attach themselves to one strong player and

feel protected and privileged. Feeling safe, these naive people ignore the advice or warnings from others in the the organization; those below them or those not connected to their circle of power.

I once overheard someone brushing off advice from those she supervised with the comment, "Oh, I don't listen to them. They're just jealous of my connection to the boss." Four months later the boss fell from power. So did she.

Another reason to help those below you is to groom your replacement. If you are the only one capable of doing your job . . . that's where you will stay.

Don't fly solo. You need a good navigator and a great ground crew. You need others to help you succeed.

Find yourself a mentor or two and . . . in turn, mentor others. If you are in a position of authority with no support you are like a general who lacks troops. There's nothing quite as powerless as a general without an army.

Splat

The path to success is not a straight line. It zigzags. As you take detours and hurdle obstacles you may feel like you are proceeding in a "two-steps forward, one-step back" fashion.

A wonderful story from the Buddhist tradition illustrates this concept.

A Master was seated under a tree one day surrounded by four of his disciples. One of the young men said, "Sir, it is time for me to go into the world seeking truth. Where do I find it?"

The Master replied, "Down that road and over that hill." So the disciple traveled down the road and over the hill. Suddenly, the remaining disciples heard a very loud "SPLAT"!

The second disciple asked the Master where he could find wisdom. He too was sent down the road and over the hill . . . "SPLAT"!

Then, the third disciple was sent down the same road and over hill to find valor . . . "SPLAT!"

The remaining disciple said, "Master, I don't understand. Everything they wanted were good, noble, honorable things. Why did you send them into 'SPLAT' ?"

The Master replied, "Because everything they wanted . . . lay three steps beyond SPLAT!"

You see, splat is abject failure. It's a bankruptcy, being fired, losing a loved one, discovering you have cancer. But so often the seeds for future success lie within splat. Splat is the experience we need to learn the lesson.

Failure is only tragic if we get stuck in splat; so a different perspective of failure is helpful. If you view failures as lessons and guideposts on your journey you can learn to appreciate them.

I believe we are a lot like guided missles. Missles are

programmed to reach their destination through a series of negative feedback. When they veer off course, the computer kicks on and directs them back.

Do you know that commercial airliners are off course 90% of the time? Through constant adjustment, negative feedback, they arrive at the right gate.

I often picture a "divine rubber mallet" in the sky that reaches down and delivers a stunning blow to let us know we're headed in the wrong direction. I have learned to pay attention to and value this whack on the side of my head.

I so admire people who can turn splat into something beneficial . . . Magic Johnson becoming a spokesperson on the subject of AIDS . . . MADD being organized after the death of a beloved daughter . . . or someone you know who loses everything and creates a better life.

The failures, disappointments, missed opportunities and detours of life, can be used to pave the way to success . . . if we have the resiliency, vision and courage to utilize "SPLAT"!

MY LONG TERM PROFESSIONAL GOALS ARE . . .

62

MY SHORT TERM OBJECTIVES ARE . . .

OBSTACLES TO OVERCOME ARE . . .

63

ALLIANCES I NEED TO ACHIVE MY GOALS AND
OBJECTIVES ARE . . .

64

MY STRENGTHS . . . MY BARTERABLE ASSETS ARE . . .

65

"ELEPHANTS" (SITUATIONS) I NEED TO WALK AROUND
AND VIEW DIFFERENTLY ARE . . .

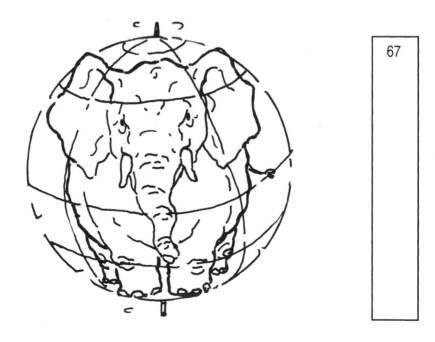

67

THIS BOOK HAS CHANGED MY PERSPECTIVES ON . . .

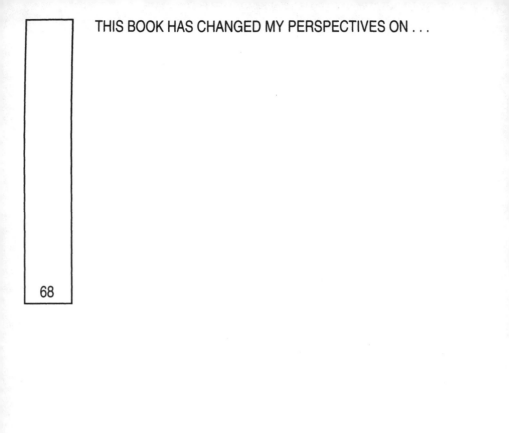

68

Billi Lee and Company, Inc. is a firm of international speakers, business consultants and seminar leaders. Each is committed to helping people work smarter by developing workplace and worldwise savvy.

For over 12 years Billi Lee and Company, Inc. has worked with clients as unique and diverse as their savvy solutions.

They have coached some of the best . . . including AT&T, MCI, Digital, Norwest Banks, FBI, CIA, Humana Hospitals, Amoco Oil, Kaiser Permanent, Kodak, ANZ Bank of Australia and the Republic of Buryat in eastern Siberia.

Billi Lee and Company, Inc. associates have demonstrated savvy and success in the real world, each with their own areas of expertise.

For more information email billilee@billilee.com.

Billi Lee is an internationally acclaimed keynote speaker loved by audiences for her dynamic, humorous and practical advice.

In addition to the many speeches and seminars she conducts Billi is an author, syndicated columnist and has been a nationally broadcast radio commentator.

Billi's perception changing seminar, "Success Savvy" has helped thousands of people become more powerful and effective. Her diverse client list spans the globe from Australia to Siberia and includes many Fortune 500 companies.

Starting with her first restaurant at the age of 19, Billi has used her entrepreneurial abilities and her love of adventure to start three restaurants, co-manage a cattle ranch, teach French in Africa, build a national sales force, advise CEO's and teach entrepreneurialism in eastern Siberia.

Billi is an entertaining provocateur, challenging her readers and audiences to take a second look at conventional wisdom, leaving no "sacred cow" untouched. Her dynamic humor delights, her fascinating stories intrigue, and her bottom-line, practical approach to the workplace helps people . . .
Get Savvy!